A History of R.A.F Station Harrowbeer Revisited

Air Ministry No 23/341
Opened August 1941 ~ Closed July 1945

Based on an original work written and published by Dennis Teague A.R.Ae.S., F.I.M.M. This 2nd edition has been further revised by Stephen Fryer on behalf of the RAF Harrowbeer Interest Group.

No. 276 Squadron ground crew pose proudly in front of a Lysander in one of the Bellman Hangars at Harrowbeer. *(photo courtesy of RAF Museum Hendon)*

Front Cover: **No.276 Squadron** line up in front of the Watch Office at Harrowbeer on the 21st March 1943, to show the resources needed to mount air sea rescue missions. Sqn Ldr Hamlyn, (No.276 Squadron's Commanding Officer) stands at the front with the rest of the air crew and support staff behind. Aircraft shown are an Avro Anson, a Spitfire MkII, and a Walrus Amphibian

ISBN: 978-0-9529922-1-9

First published by S C Fryer and © RAF Harrowbeer Interest Group 2010
2nd edition published June 2014

Acknowledgements

This is the 2nd edition of this book and it has had some corrections and updates from the first revision published in 2010. As well as acknowledging those who helped Dennis write the original, I would like to thank the following people.

All the members of the Harrowbeer Interest Group, including Mike, Lucy & Francis Hayes for checking the various ORBs. Peter Davey and Bernie Steed for all the technical corrections. Darell Jago (who also helped Dennis with the original manuscript) for corrections and supplying some of the original photos. Chris Woodcock for additional details to do with 193 Squadron. Brian Salt for cleaning up many of the pictures and for constantly re-reading the draft copies looking for typing errors. And to my wife Claire for putting up with me spending hours at the computer.

There are lots of other people who have chipped in with facts, including Jerry Brewer, Colin Foster, RAF Museum Hendon and of course the National Archives at Kew.

And finally the Teague Family for allowing us to revise his work.

Stephen Fryer

Technical Information on RAF Harrowbeer

OS Grid Reference: SX513679   **Lat/Long:** 50° 29' 32.90 N 4° 5'49.80 W

Height above sea level: 650 ft   **Airfield Code:** QB

Runways: length/width - all were surfaced with Asphalt

Runway No.1: QDM 11/29 3840 ft x 150 ft

Runway No.2: QDM 17/35 3345 ft x 150 ft

Runway No.3: QDM 05/23 2736 ft x 150 ft

Airfield opened: 15th Aug 1941   **Airfield closed operationally:** 31st July 1945

Airfield remained on "Care & Maintenance" until 1962

Dispersal (blast or 'E') bays: 12   **Hangars:** 2 x Bellman T2 and 8 x Blister

The following abbreviations are used throughout this book:

Plt Off - Pilot Officer, **Fg Off** - Flying Officer, **Flt Lt** - Flight Lieutenant, Cpl - Corporal
Sqn Ldr - Squadron Leader, **Wg Cdr** - Wing Commander, **Gp Capt** - Group Captain.
Sgt - Sergeant, **Flt Sgt** - Flight Sergeant, **WO** - Warrant Officer, **S/O** - Section Officer
CO - Commanding Officer, **Lt.Col.** - Lieutenant Colonel, **LACW** - Leading Aircraftwoman

DFC - Distinguished Flying Cross
DFM - Distinguished Flying Medal

ATC - Air Training Corps (also know as the Air Cadets)
ORB - Operations Record Book (a daily diary of Squadron or Airfield events)
QDM - a 'Q' code for Direction Magnetic

Preface

In the 1980s, Dennis Teague wrote and published a book on R.A.F. Harrowbeer, a wartime airfield at Yelverton in Devon. This book had long been out of print when in 2010, and with the kind permission of Dennis's family, the RAF Harrowbeer Interest Group undertook to update the book, with revised photographs and updated text. Unfortunately, many of the photos that Dennis originally used were not available as he did not record exactly who he had borrowed them from and so they were substituted with new ones from the RAF Harrowbeer Interest Group collection.
(*Stephen Fryer 2014*)

Here is a section of the preface from the original book:

"In the early days of the War, I was an A.T.C. cadet and greeted the new aerodrome at Yelverton with great excitement as it held promise of different types of aircraft than those which operated from Roborough. I spent many hours there and any spare time that I had watching the fighters assembling for take off or returning from sweeps across the Channel. Unless one actually experienced the sight of a fighter unit formating, it is hard to describe. Prior to moving off, each mighty Typhoon was cartridge-started and one could watch the pilot and ground crew firing up. A bang was followed by a puff of blue grey smoke until at last the huge four-bladed propeller churned around and the massive engine spluttered into life, accompanied usually by a streak of flame and cloud of smoke. Each aircraft squeaked and groaned its way around until it was positioned for take off. Receiving the signal for the off, it roared down the runway and up into a sharp bank following the others and would join up in a large circle of as many as 30 planes and whilst the last ones were taking off the pack would be droning around Burrator to Tavistock. Finally, they would all form into a wedge shape and head off to the South East and the targets in the Channel Islands. Harrowbeer was an active drome and, whilst not on a par with some of the other bases along the South Coast, it was always the home of at least one visiting Squadron in addition to the Air Sea Rescue unit and Communication units. It was very much multi-national and generally popular with the aircrews. During the war it served the country well and now remains in peace having reverted to scrubland with only a stone to mark that it ever existed."

Later he added an additional note:

"Shortly after my book "Aviation in South West Britain 1909-1979" had been published in 1982, I was approached by Mrs. O. Meggy who requested permission to use data from the book in a small booklet that she was preparing on Harrowbeer and she told me of the plans to erect a stone memorial to the wartime users of the airfield. Later on she told me of the information that she had collected and her hope to have it printed. Sadly Mrs. Meggy is no longer with us and I am therefore including her data with mine so that her ambition may be fulfilled."

Dennis Teague (1928—1998)

Dennis was a Navy, Army, Railway and Aircraft historian. He was also a writer, photographer and prolific modeller of aircraft, ships, army tanks and personnel. His main interest was with the preservation of aircraft and the recording of West Country aviation events and airfields before their history was lost

Dennis Teague

Harrowbeer airfield as seen from above showing the distinctive crossed 'A' plan of the runways. The layout of these is as follows: Runway No.1 (QDM 11/29) runs from below Yelverton roundabout (seen at the top) straight down the picture. Runway No.2 (QDM 17/35) crosses Runway No.1 from left to right and Runway No.3 (QDM 05/23) runs from the roundabout to the right of the picture. The Great Western Railway line is at the top of the picture, running under Yelverton roundabout and the distinctive curve of the Princetown Branch can also be seen.

Royal Air Force Station Harrowbeer, Devon

There can be few other airfields, if any, that were built with the rubble of the place they were designed to protect from enemy bombing, but this was the case with Harrowbeer. Situated at Yelverton, nine miles North of Plymouth on the road to Tavistock, one could be forgiven if you went right past it today without ever knowing that it had existed. It is here, as the road approaches Yelverton Roundabout, that you will first see a large rock outcrop (the famous Roborough Rock) and, further on the same side, partly hidden by trees, some grassy mounds. These mounds are the remains of the aircraft dispersal bays of Harrowbeer airfield and more can be seen if one turns left by the Rock and drives towards Crapstone and Buckland Monachorum.

Indeed, most drivers will be unaware that the roads hereabouts (and Yelverton roundabout itself) were constructed by the RAF to divert traffic around the new airfield. Today, it hardly seems possible that a busy airfield even existed on this open moorland and, that a very bitter conflict was waged post-war when it was proposed as a replacement for Roborough, Plymouth's commercial airport (now also closed). The latter is more surprising given that Harrowbeer was actually chosen as the preferred option to replace Roborough back in the late 1930s.

The construction of RAF Harrowbeer started in late 1940 and work progressed swiftly to clear the scrubland and lay down the standard 'A' type configuration of runways. Opposition to it seems to have been minimal when faced with the prospect of invasion and the airfield opened officially on the 15th August 1941, although it was far from complete. The Plymouth blitz of 1941 saw the almost total destruction of the City Centre and a large quantity of the subsequent rubble was brought out and used in the construction of some of the new roads, taxi-ways and to complete the runways. The aforementioned Roborough Rock, situated at the southern end of two of the runways, was topped with an obstruction light as a warning to pilots.

No.193 Squadron: Typhoon (DP-E) of 'B' Flight, photographed at Harrowbeer in 1943. Pilot F/O Vernon-Jarvis is in the centre, with Airframe Mechanic Philips (left) and Engine Mechanic R E Tudball (right). The name of the person holding the propeller isn't known.

The first building to be constructed was a corrugated iron blister hangar on land adjacent to the Rock. This, with a large house, which still exists today called Ravenscroft, was the start of occupation. The house became the station HQ and was fully occupied until the end of the war. It was then vacated and for several years was the target of the 'Polish gold' hunters. A story had got around that when the Polish Forces set up in Britain they had brought with them vast amounts of gold and silver objects from their churches and had buried them on one of the British airfields that they served on. The result of this rumour was amazing, as everywhere the Poles had been, small groups of diggers were to be noted leaving a trail of destruction behind them! In the South West this included, Culmhead, Exeter, Predannack, Davidstow Moor and, of course, Harrowbeer.

At this point in the original text, Dennis Teague mentions *"Another semi-circular hangar was erected with bombing dispersals near the Rock and the control tower more or less completed the South Western corner. Some stores were built up in the North West corner and a sick quarters organised but on a small scale"* The Harrowbeer Interest Group (HIG) has been unable to find any record of the second hangar described but this may refer to the blister hangars constructed later near Ravenscroft. The Control Tower mentioned is now Knightstone Tea Rooms but this was originally a house called Victoria Lodge. It was converted by the RAF for use as the airfield's control tower prior to the construction of a purpose built one on the other side of the airfield.

The first officially recorded aircraft to land at Harrowbeer was a Blenheim Mk.I on the 31st August 1941, and this was parked outside the blister hangar by the Rock. A few days later several more arrived, these being Blenheim Mk.IVFs of No.500 Squadron. They were fighters and used on anti-shipping and intruder operations over airfields in occupied France.

The size of the airfield at that time, compared to the number of aircraft using it, was out of all proportions. However, all this was to change and quite large aircraft did land, usually on weather diversions or emergency landings. Harrowbeer was not a bomber base and the sightings of Halifax, Stirling, Lancaster and B17 'Flying Fortress' aircraft gave rise to very strange accounts of hundreds of American bombers taking off, and even reports from crews who state that they flew operations in bombers from here (they turned out to be Coastal Command Liberators from Chivenor, North Devon). The station at no time operated bombers, although one Halifax did manage to force land right alongside the main road near the Rock. One large transport Harrow used to fly in and out on communication flights, as did many Oxford and Anson aircraft.

The first fighter squadrons arrive

In October 1941, No.130 (Punjab) Squadron brought their Spitfires to Harrowbeer and they stayed until November. No.276 Air Sea Rescue Squadron was formed at Harrowbeer on the 21st October and they operated Anson, Defiant, Spitfire, Lysander and Walrus aircraft. October also saw the arrival of No.302 (City of Poznan) Squadron, a Polish Squadron commanded by Sqn Ldr Kowalski, that soon had their Hurricanes replaced with Spitfire VBs. The Squadron had previously served at Churchstanton (later renamed Culmhead in December 1943 to avoid confusion with Church Fenton in Yorkshire) on the Somerset border with Devon. They were similar to several other RAF Squadrons, which were made up with pilots from many nations who had escaped the German occupation. The West Country was host to Polish, Czech, French and Belgian Squadrons, plus units from the Dutch, Norwegian, Royal Australian, Rhodesian, Royal Canadian and Royal New Zealand Squadrons, together with the U.S. Navy/Army Air Forces. All these were part of an impressive total of 286 overseas units known to have served in this country at one time or another during the War and shortly afterwards.

Sqdn no	Code letters	date from:	date to:	aircraft type	from airfield:	to airfield:
26	XC	7/1/45	22/1/45	Mustang IV	Exeter	North Weald
26	XC	Apr 45	May 45	Spitfire XIV	North Weald	Chilboton
64	SH	22/6/44	30/8/44	Spitfire VB Spitfire IX	Deanland	Bradwell Bay
126	5J	3/7/44	29/8/44	Spitfire IX	Culmhead	Bradwell Bay
130	PJ	25/10/41	30/11/41	Spitfire II	Portreath	Warmwell
131	NX	24/3/44	24/5/44	Spitfire VII	Colerne	Culmhead
165	GT	20/6/44	22/6/44	Spitfire IX	Predannack	Detling
175	HH	10/10/42	9/12/42	Hurricane IIB	Warmwell	Gatwick
183	HF	5/6/43	4/8/43	Typhoon 1A	Colerne	Tangmere
193	DP	18/12/42	20/2/44	Typhoon 1B	(Formed)	Fairlop
263	HE	20/2/43	15/3/43	Whirlwind F1	Warmwell	Warmwell
263	HE	19/3/43	19/6/44	Typhoon	Warmwell	Bolt Head
266	ZH	21/9/43	7/3/44	Typhoon 1B	Exeter	Bolt Head
266	ZH	12/3/44	15/3/44	Typhoon 1B	Bolt Head	Acklington
275	PV	10/1/45	15/2/45	Walrus	Exeter	(Disbanded)
276	AQ	21/10/41	3/4/44	Lysander Walrus	(Formed)	Portreath
276	TQ	21/10/41	3/4/44	Defiant Spitfire Anson	(Formed)	Portreath
302 (Polish)	WX	7/10/41	7/5/42	Hurricane Spitfire VB	Churchstanton	Heston
312 (Czech)	DU	2/5/42	10/10/42	Spitfire VB	Fairwood Common	Churchstanton
329 (Free French)	5A	25/5/45 19/6/45	16/6/45 14/7/45	Spitfire IX	Skaebrae Dreux	Dreux Fairwood
610	DW	24/5/44	?/6/44	Spitfire XIV	Bolt Head	West Malling
611	FY	23/6/44	3/7/44	Spitfire LF VB	DeanLand	Predannack
838 F.A.A. R.N.		20/4/44	8/8/44	Fairey Swordfish	Machrihanish	Worthy Down

Main Squadrons associated with and operating from RAF Harrowbeer 1941-45

The above list, whilst in no way definitive, shows the main Squadrons that were stationed at Harrowbeer between 1941 and 1945. Many other Squadrons arrived at Harrowbeer and stayed for anything from a day to a few weeks.

By the start of 1942, with building work still in progress, Harrowbeer began to resemble an operational Station. When No.302 Squadron left in April, Sqn Ldr Cermak and No.312 (Czech) Squadron, equipped with Spitfire VBs, arrived to replace them and they stayed until the beginning of October. The Czechs were fearless pilots and were engaged with defending South coast towns from 'tip and run' raiders as well as taking part in fighter sweeps across the Channel and into France.

Early October 1942 saw the arrival of No.175 with Hurricane IIBs, which were the fighter-bomber version of these famous aircraft (nick-named Hurribombers) and almost at once they were engaged in attacks upon enemy shipping. Targets in the Channel Islands and along the French coast were also subjected to low level strikes. One of the Squadron's

A Whirlwind aircraft of 263 Squadron, possibly at Harrowbeer in 1941. Note the construction vehicles in the background. Building work at Harrowbeer started in late 1940 and went on right into 1942. The markings on this aircraft indicate that it was photographed between April and September 1941, possibly after making an emergency landing as its right hand engine appears to be stopped.

successes came when they intercepted three E-boats. The E-boat was a very high speed torpedo boat that had earned a deadly reputation around the coasts and they had wreaked havoc amongst, not only the merchant shipping, but their escorts as well. Well armed, they engaged without fear and when the Hurribombers were directed on to three of them, the odds were against the aircraft. The E-boats were armed with one 37mm cannon, plus one twin 20mm and one single 20mm cannon and each of the three boats put up a barrage of fire, heavier, and at greater range than the Hurricanes could match. Thus it was no mean feat of the 175 Sqn pilots to bomb and sink two; and badly damage the third of the E-boats.

On December 18th, 1942, No.193 Squadron was formed at Harrowbeer. It was to be equipped with the new Typhoon fighter and was to remain for another two years. The Typhoon was a very fine aircraft but suffered a high casualty rate due to an engine that failed to come up to expectations and a tail section that had a nasty habit of breaking off in flight until it was modified. The Typhoon was a snub-nosed design with all the weight up in the front and in the early days this made the take off and landing very difficult to cope with and yet, once mastered, the 'Tiffy' could be flown superbly. It did not meet its design specification as a high altitude interceptor and so was tried out in the reverse role of a low level fighter-bomber. The early machines had 12 x 0.303in machine guns but these were later replaced by 4x20mm cannon and thus a new and probably the most deadly strike aircraft was born. Later still, 8 x 60lb rockets or two underwing bombs of either 250lb or 500lb were added and these, delivered at high speed, took their toll of shipping, installations and vehicles alike. Harrowbeer's aircraft were to be engaged on this type of work for the next couple of years until 1944.

Unfortunately, several of Harrowbeer's Typhoon aircraft came to grief, one hitting the tower of nearby St Paul's Church in Yelverton in May 1944, and five others crashed on Dartmoor. On the airfield itself, four more were lost during take off and landing and many more failed to return from missions over enemy-held territory.

1943 to 1944

In February 1943, No.263 Squadron arrived with their Westland Whirlwind aircraft. Since their formation, No.263 had served at Charmy Down, Bolt Head, Exeter, Portreath/ Nanskuke and St Eval. The Whirlwind fighter was an excellent design, popular with most pilots but dogged with engine troubles and was not produced in great numbers (in fact a total of only 117 aircraft were actually built). It performed well in the fighter-bomber role

No.175 Squadron: Two Hurricane IIBs of No.175 Squadron parked in a dispersal bay near Whistley. These aircraft were the fighter-bomber version of the Hurricane and were nicknamed 'Hurribombers'. Note the Bellman hangar in the background with its doors open.

too and, escorted by fighters, played a useful part in strike attacks. During February they made several anti-shipping attacks off the northern coast of France and when, during March, the squadron converted to the Typhoon, many pilots expressed mixed feelings about losing the Whirlwinds.

Harrowbeer has often been dubbed a Typhoon station although that is not strictly true. However, during 1943, there were more of these aircraft at Harrowbeer than any other, so it is easy to see how this perception came about. Together with No.193 Squadron, Nos. 263, 183 (Gold Coast) and 266 Squadrons all flew Typhoons from Harrowbeer at various times during that year.

In May 1943, Mustangs of No.414 Squadron, of the Royal Canadian Air Force, arrived with a ground attack and photo-reconnaissance role. The Station had by now become fully operational and a great deal of activity took place which now causes considerable difficulty to ascertain. Buildings continued to be erected around the northern limits and then United States Naval staff arrived, but for what reason still remains unclear. They were visited from time-to-time by their Catalina PBY 5A aircraft and an unidentified communications flight of US aircraft were based near the Rock, comprising Oxford and Spitfire aircraft with US markings. During the period 1943-45 a large number of American light aircraft used the Station and many operational types diverted to Harrowbeer until weather conditions improved at their home bases. Dennis Teague recalls seeing four all-white Hudson aircraft belonging to the Royal Canadian Air Force that were parked just inside the fence at Leg O' Mutton. The unit is thought to have been No.407 Squadron.

In addition to the US aircraft which sometimes had to divert to Harrowbeer, there was also the occasional RAF bomber that landed there. On the 28th February, 1943, a Halifax was returning to its base at Gravely, but badly damaged, the pilot, Sqn Ldr Dean, decided to divert to Harrowbeer. On landing however, the aircraft overshot the runway and careered across the current A386 and onto the rough ground beyond, only stopping when its undercarriage collapsed. Within hours the next day, the rumour was spread that it was one of first of many four-engined aircraft to take up residence. However, W7906 of No.35 Squadron departed on several low loaders.

Another myth was that several feet were removed from the top of the Rock itself, the reason being given was so that fully laden bombers could clear the top. Transport and communication aircraft were quite large, but did not have much trouble operating from Harrowbeer and quite a few of the twin-engined aircraft of Bomber Command and the USAAF could be seen from time-to-time on the station. Boston, Havoc, Marauder, Hampden, Wellington and Blenheim aircraft all made short stays. A Stirling dwarfed everything else but even that was overshadowed when the US Liberator transports started using the Station along with PBY-5A Catalina aircraft from Dunkeswell.

Spitfires Everywhere

In 1944, Harrowbeer saw a complete change of aircraft as the Typhoons departed to make way for squadron after squadron of Spitfires. Like all stations, Harrowbeer in 1944 was top line to support the allied invasion of Europe. The date was kept secret but there was no way of covering up that it was only a matter of time. The fighter bombers moved away nearer to where they were going to be needed and a mass of fighters gathered in the South West to provide cover and destroy any enemy aircraft attacks. Although Coastal Command and the allied navies had virtually eliminated the major threat to the ships crossing the Channel, no chance could be taken and so Fleet Air Arm anti-submarine aircraft started being deployed to RAF bases. The big build up was under way.

February had seen No.193 Squadron leave with their Typhoons, and they were followed in March by No.266 Squadron and in April, No.276 (ASR) Squadron moved to Bolt Head. These were replaced by No.131 (County of Kent) Squadron with Spitfire VIIs (who stayed until May) and the ensuing months saw a flood of other Spitfire Squadrons make short deployments to Harrowbeer. On one occasion forty-eight of them took off to attack enemy targets in France, along with bomb-carrying Typhoons from Bolt Head. Likewise, the Spitfire Mk VIIs of No.131 Squadron joined with No.340 (Ille de France) Free French Squadron for similar raids during April.

The build-up to D-Day brought No.610 Squadron, with Mk XIV Spitfires, and the Typhoons of No.263 Squadron to Harrowbeer and on the 6th June they attacked shipping targets in the Channel Islands. In the following days they flew over 100 sorties in support of the ground forces fighting on the Normandy beaches. Later in the month, Nos.1, 64, 165 and 611 Spitfire Squadrons arrived at Harrowbeer and during July 1944, No.126 Squadron stayed for a month with Spitfire IXs. By August 1944, the fighting in France had moved inland and it was taking longer for aircraft from Harrowbeer to reach the front line and so, with Harrowbeer's role almost at an end, the Station was closed.

A Mustang Mk 1 (AM251) of No.414 Sqdn of the Royal Canadian Air Force at Harrowbeer in 1943. The Squadron had a ground attack and photo-reconnaissance role and the black 'dot' above the letter 'O' is where a 5" camera was seated within the fuselage.

However, this closure was not final and Harrowbeer re-opened in January 1945 and then in February, No.691 Squadron arrived with Oxford and Vengeance aircraft and they stayed until the end of August. They were joined by No.329 (Free French) Squadron, with Spitfire IXs, who had the honour of being the last operational fighter unit to use the airfield.

Accidents at the Station

It is inevitable that any airfield would have its share of accidents and crashes. The first fatality at Harrowbeer was in December 1941, when a Spitfire of No.302 Squadron swung to the left on take-off and hit a stationary Spitfire (also of No.302 Squadron) killing one of the ground crew. A more serious accident happened in July 1942, when during take-off, a Blenheim hit a Commer van carrying personnel of No.276 Squadron, killing four of the occupants of the van. The Blenheim was able to make a circuit before crash-landing on the runway. In November 1942, a Defiant crashed on landing near Leg O' Mutton. Sadly the crew were killed but customers in a nearby café had a lucky escape when one of the plane's wheels crashed through the window. In May 1943, another Defiant was involved in the Station's most serious accident when, during take-off, it struck a lorry carrying members of a local Pioneer Corps who were visiting the airfield. Three of them were killed and six injured. The Defiant crashed, injuring the pilot.

There were many accidents caused by cartridge starters, (used for starting the engines of Spitfires and Typhoons etc) which, after more than three attempts, gave a real danger of fire. Several aircraft skidded off the runways and tipped over, plus there were landing and take-off failures. Typhoons, although excellent in the ground attack role, were prone to engine troubles. Examples of this being aircraft DN470 and DN510 of No.193 Squadron which both crashed on landing. 'Paddy' Pringle, of No.263 Squadron was killed when his Typhoon hit the tower of St Paul's Church in Yelverton, in May 1944. Another Typhoon of No.263 Squadron crashed at Launceston in June 1944. No.183 Squadron lost three Typhoon aircraft in accidents; JP404 spun into the ground, JP388 was damaged in an overshot when landing, and JP393 burst a tyre on take off. No.266 Squadron lost JP962 which overshot and JR221 which crashed near Tavistock. A Mosquito of No.406 Squadron crashed and exploded near Ravenscroft and several Spitfires and visiting aircraft also came to grief. Probably the saddest loss was when two young airmen tossed a coin for one of them to have the chance to fly in No.276 Squadron's Lysander on a search and rescue mission. The aircraft took off and was never seen or heard of again.

Today, the crews of these aircraft and also those that failed to return from operations are remembered on the stone memorial located at Leg O' Mutton.

The Closing of RAF Harrowbeer

RAF Harrowbeer's operational life ended at the end of July 1945 but there was to be one more starring role for the airfield when, two days after the Station officially closed, on the 2nd August, a strange chain of events was to put Harrowbeer on the map as far as the press were concerned. It all started at Gatow, in Germany, when the Heads of State that had attended the world-shaping Potsdam Conference in Berlin were making their way home.

US President Harry S Truman was routed from Gatow to St Mawgan, in Cornwall, which was the principal transit base for UK-USA transatlantic flights. His aircraft, a Douglas VC-54C called 'Sacred Cow', departed Gatow at 08:05, ten minutes after the first aircraft carrying the Secretary of State, James Byrnes. A third aircraft, with the remainder of the party, followed. Bad weather now took a hand in the proceedings. St Mawgan was closed because of fog, so the party of VIPs was diverted to Harrowbeer and the President's aircraft touched down at 09:40. Unfortunately, because the reception party was at St Mawgan, there was only one officer, Lt. Col. Dewitt Greer, at Harrowbeer to welcome the President when he landed.

King George VI was onboard HMS Renown at anchor in Plymouth Sound, together with the USS Augusta and USS Philadelphia. President Truman boarded the USS Augusta at 11:20 and, at 12:35, the President, Secretary Byrnes and Admiral Leahy left USS Augusta for HMS Renown to call upon his Majesty and were accorded the highest honours. A return visit followed at 15:04 when the King, together with the Earl of Halifax and Sir Allen Lascalles called on the President. The King left at 15:34 and fifteen minutes later the ships got under way.

Harrowbeer's recent past

In the years that followed, Harrowbeer was used in a number of ways. ATC cadets spent time there and gliding was also undertaken. Many local people too, learnt to drive on the tarmac runways. Finally, in the 1960s, following a failed attempt to make Harrowbeer the new Plymouth Airport, the remaining buildings were demolished and the runways torn up.

Today, only the dispersal bays and concrete hut bases remain for the visitor to see, but the legacy of the old Airfield has not been forgotten. The Harrowbeer Interest Group formed in 2004 and has erected three interpretation boards at various points around the airfield. The Group is busily involved with recording Harrowbeer's wartime history and has a website, www.rafharrowbeer.co.uk, which has allowed people all over the world to read about its history.

More recently, in 2011, the 70th Anniversary of the opening of the Airfield was celebrated with two days of events and flying displays from an Air Sea Rescue Sea King, a Swordfish from the Royal Naval Historic Flight and a Hurricane and Spitfire from the Battle of Britain Memorial Flight.

No.193 Squadron: *From L to R:* Fg Off Peter Thorne, FLt Sgt Eddie Richardson, Fg Off Vernon-Jarvis, Fg Off Ray Hulbert, Sgt Reg Roberts, Sgt Rod Davidge, Flt Sgt Tommy Lowe, and Sgt Phil Murton. The dog was called Bonnie and belonged to Vernon-Jarvis.

1981 Stone Memorial

In 1981, a granite memorial was erected at Harrowbeer, near Leg o' Mutton, as a tribute to all who served there. It reads:

RAF Harrowbeer Operational 1941-1949

"From this station flew pilots of many commonwealth and allied countries, including Britain, Canada, Czechoslovakia, France, Poland and the United States of America. With the support of their ground crews and airfield defence units. This stone is in memory of all who served here and especially of those who gave their lives."

The photograph shows the stone being unveiled by the Station's first Commander, Group Captain the Honourable H. E. Ward, together with Lt Col R Middleton, on the 15th August 1981, which was the fortieth anniversary of the opening of the station.

RAF Harrowbeer Interest Group Interpretation Boards

In 2006, the Harrowbeer Interest Group erected three interpretation boards on the airfield so that visitors can better understand the area's war-time history.

This one stands in front of the dispersal bay near the Rock. Knightstone Tea Rooms, the original Control Tower (or Watch Office) can be seen in the distance.

Ravenscroft

This was the Station's HQ, Officers' Mess and quarters and is seen here as it looked during its wartime role.

It is now a private nursing home and has been much renovated since the war. It has also had several extensions added to it over the years giving it a much changed appearance.

CO's Office

This sparsely furnished room at Ravenscroft was the Station Commander's office and, no doubt, will hold memories for many ranks. For it was from here that news of returning aircraft, together with reports of lost aircraft and crews was made known.

In the Cockpit

Sqn Ldr Hamlyn, CO of No.276 Sqn, from December 1942 to September 1943, is seen here sitting in the cockpit of his Spitfire.

The photograph clearly shows the headrest behind the pilot and the type of headgear worn, with its oxygen mask.

Note too, the rear-view mirror (top left) fitted as an after-thought to Spitfires and Hurricanes to give the pilot a view behind him.

No.276 (Air Sea Rescue) Squadron

Loading an ASR Spitfire IIC

No.276 Squadron's Spitfire IIC is loaded with a dinghy and smoke flares prior to a rescue mission from Harrowbeer.

The smoke flares would give the downed pilot's position and indicate the wind direction for the Walrus to land.

A Rescue Celebration

Officers and personnel of No.276 Squadron stand on the steps of Ravenscroft to celebrate their 100th rescue which had already risen to 106 by the time this photo was taken.

Rescued by a Walrus

A Walrus amphibian taxis up to a pilot in his dinghy.

It is often forgotten that this ungainly aircraft was built by the same company that built the beautiful Spitfire!

Air Sea Rescue was a very important part of the role of the Station and many Harrowbeer pilots owed their lives to the work of No.276 Squadron during the war

No.276 Squadron: *Above:* The view from No.276 Squadron's office window in Ravenscroft. A Walrus and Defiant are in the dispersal pen and a Spitfire is parked opposite. Runway No.3 can clearly be seen running right to left in the distance, but harder to spot is Runway No.2 which crosses behind the parked Spitfire. Unsuccessful attempts were made to camouflage this runway with coloured rubber chippings (possibly why it appears darker in this photograph).

Below: Ground Crew prepare canisters and a smoke bomb for dropping from a Lysander.

HARROWBEER WING SCORE	From 31/8 To 1/9 Incl.			
TARGETS ATTACKED	**126 Sq**	**64 Sq**		**TOTAL** WING
E/A DEST.	3FW¹⁹⁰ 5ME10⁹	2 ME109	611	3FW190 8 ME109 1 DO217(G)
Pr. Dest.	1 UTE (G) 1 ME109			1 U.TE(G) 1 ME109
DAM.	2 ME109 4 JU88 (G)			4 JU88 (G) 2 ME109
LOCOS.	16	2	5	23
RAIL TRUCKS DEST + DAM	40	79	30	149
M.T. Vehicles DEST + DAM	78	54	47	179
A.F.V.S.	1	—	7	8
Shipping DEST + DAM (TONS)	210	630	300	1140
Installations				

Above: An unusual photo of the Harrowbeer 'scoreboard' in late August 1944 showing the successes of two squadrons in late August. No.64 Sqn spent two months at Harrowbeer, whereas No.611 Sqn swapped places with No.126 Sqn during early July.

Below: **No.193 Squadron:** Sgt 'Sammy' Samuels at the controls of a Typhoon named 'Salome' ready for another sortie from Harrowbeer sometime in 1943

No.302 (City of Poznan) Squadron

No.302 Squadron were visited by the Polish President in exile, President Raczkowski, in November 1941, when he presented medals to aircrew.

In the top picture he is seen acknowledging the Polish flag on arrival at Harrowbeer and then above he takes the salute at a march past by the Squadron on one of the runways. In the picture (right) he is seen presenting an airman with his medal.

Photos courtesy of the Polish Institute and Sikorski Museum

Left: Pilots of 'B' Flight seen at readiness outside their dispersal hut at Harrowbeer in the Summer of 1942.

Right: Flt Sgt Frank Mares is seen running to his Spitfire at Harrowbeer in 1942. His parachute is hanging on the wing in readiness for a speedy take off.

At a ceremony at Harrowbeer on the 26th September 1942, Frank was awarded the Distinguished Flying Medal (DFM) by Gp Capt Orlebar, Commanding Officer of No.10 Group. Frank was the first Czech Pilot to be awarded a DFM.

Left: Two groundcrew watch as a Spitfire takes off from Harrowbeer.

No.312 Squadron: *Above:* Flt Sgt M. A. (Tony) Liskutin sits in his Spitfire VB awaiting take off sometime in May or June 1942.

Below: A Spitfire is re-armed in one of the dispersal bays. Note the Watch Office and Bellman Hangar in the background.

No.193 Squadron: *Above & Below:* Pilots of 'A' Flight at readiness outside their dispersal hut at Axtown on the western side of the airfield.

Above: L to R: Sgt Reg Roberts, Sgt Phil Murton, F/O Eddie Richardson, F/Sgt Eddie Vernon-Jarvis, Sgt Ian Ross.

Below: L to R: Sgt Ian Ross, Sgt Ed Barff. F/O Eddie Vernon-Jarvis, P/O 'Killy' Kilpatrick, Sgt Rod Davidge, P/O John Hill, F/Sgt Eddie Richardson, P/O Bill Switzer, Sgt Pattinson

No.193 Squadron: The Squadron was formed at Harrowbeer on the 18th December 1942 and stayed until early 1944. In the above picture they are seen in a commemorative photo taken on the 16th Oct 1943, following the presentation to the Squadron by the Brazilian Ambassador, of nine Hawker Typhoon aircraft which had been purchased by the Fellowship of the Bellows of Brazil. In its early form, the Typhoon was not a reliable aircraft, suffering numerous problems.

Senior Officers at RAF Harrowbeer

Above: Wg Cdr J Butterworth, (2nd left) CO of the Station during 1943 & 1944, with Sqn Ldr MacKenzie (left) CO of No.64 Sqn, and Sqn Ldr Plazis DFC (right), CO of No.126 Sqn and Wg Cdr H Bird-Wilson (2nd right) in August 1944.

Below: Wg Cdr H Bird-Wilson (right) with Sqn Ldr Mackenzie and Sqn Ldr Plazis.

Visitors to RAF Harrowbeer

The Airfield has had a number of high-profile visitors over the years.

Right: 16th Oct 1943. The Brazilian Ambassador Dr J.J. Moniz de Aragão inspects No.193 Sqn during his visit to present the squadron with nine Hawker Typhoon aircraft which had been paid for by the South American based Fellowship of the Bellows of Brazil.

Right: Two days after Harrowbeer was officially closed in 1945, President Truman's plane was diverted to the airfield due to fog at St Mawgan.

(L to R: S/O Eira Buckland-Jones, President Harry S Truman, Cpl Clarice Turner, Sec of State James S Byrnes, LACW Audley Bartlett.

Below: in 1942, the Duke of Kent visited No.312 Sqn whilst they were at Harrowbeer. Of note is the fact that someone has tried to write the names of all the people in the photograph.

Above: **No.193 Squadron**. Sgt Reg Roberts (wearing the lifejacket) stands by his Typhoon DP-V (DN386) with his rigger and fitter at Harrowbeer, probably during 1943.

Below: **No.838 Squadron**. No.838 Squadron (Fleet Air Arm) was equipped with rocket firing Swordfish aircraft at Harrowbeer. Here, J Steward, E Townsend and William Locke smile for the photographer possibly prior to flying a mission, as two of them are dressed in immersion suits.

No. 130 Squadron. During 1941, the Squadron was based at Harrowbeer from late October to the end of November. During this time they switched from flying Spitfire IIAs to Spitfire Vbs. The squadron was engaged on shipping patrols, fighter sweeps and bomber escort duties. Seen here is Spitfire Vb PJ-C Ad370. In the background (right) can be seen the shops, etc, at Leg O Mutton, meaning the aircraft is in one of the dispersal bays on the A386 side of the airfield.

Nos 64 & 126 Squadron were at Harrowbeer during July and August 1944. They formed the "Harrowbeer Wing" and flew Spitfire Mk IXs on sweeps over the Channel and Northern France.

There were many unfortunate accidents at Harrowbeer. This Typhoon of No 183 Squadron ended up upside-down at the Yelverton end of Runway No.3 on 15th July 1943. The properties (back right) still stand today, enabling us to exactly pinpoint the scene of this unfortunate mishap.

On the 16th October 2009, the Brazilian Air Attaché, Col Cesar Estevam Barbosa, came to Harrowbeer to unveil a plaque commemorating the link between No 193 Squadron and the Bellows of Brazil. The plaque was the idea of Brazilian businessman Carlos Thompson Motta who had been researching the history of the Bellows organisation. The date for the unveiling was chosen specifically because it was 66 years ago that the Brazilian Ambassador came to Harrowbeer to present Typhoons to No. 193 Sqn (see page 24).

Above: Col Barbosa is seen shaking hands with Percy Beake, DFC, AE, a former 193 Sqn pilot who was present at the 1943 ceremony. David Ince, DFC (right) also flew with 193 Sqn.

Below: details of the plaque which has been fixed to the wall of Knightstone Tea Rooms.

193 SQUADRON (BELLOWS OF BRAZIL)
RAF HARROWBEER 16 OCTOBER 1943

**In Honour of all Pilots and Ground Crew of 193 Squadron
who served on this Station during World War II
and in rememberance of those who sacrificed their lives.**

**To the efforts of the civilians who made the Fellowship of the Bellows a reality
and an example of Friendship and Solidarity between
Brazil and Great Britain.**

Personnel of 193 Squadron

A flight
F/Lt. P .H. Beake. Officer Commanding.
F/O. F. H. HULBERT. A. F. C.
F/O. A. W. KILPATRICK.
F/O. W. A. SWITZER.
F/O. E. B. WALLACE.
F/O. J. L. W. HILL.
P/O. R. W. DAVIDGE.
P/O. T. LOWE.
W/O. N. I. FREAKLEY.
W/O. E. RICHARDSON.
F/Sgt. I. D. ROSS.
F/Sgt. P. G. MURTON.
Sgt. J. R. KING-MEGGAT.
Sgt. G. E. LANGILLE.

S/Ldr. G. W. PETRE. COMMANDING OFFICER.

F/Lt. G. M. T. WEBB. Engineering Officer.
F/Lt. W. E. CHAPMAN. Medical Officer.
F/O. H. L. JONES. Adjutant.
F/O. D. S. BEEDIE. Intelligence Officer.

F/Lt. D. V. C. COTES PREEDY. G. M. (Supernumerary)

B flight
F/Lt. J. M. CRABB. Officer Commanding.
F/Lt. G. E. CASSIE.
F/O. J. A. INGLIS.
F/O. J. A. PRESSLAND.
F/O. J. W. DARLING.
P/O. R. G. MACLEOD.
P/O. E. STATTERS.
P/O. M. SOBLE.
W/O. G. L. BILZ.
F/Sgt. N. K. BALE.
F/Sgt. J. BRADSHAW.
F/Sgt. J. McCARTNEY.
F/Sgt. C. C. GILMOUR.
Sgt. G. E. GOUGH.
Sgt. R. VAN-CUYLENBURG.
Sgt. H. W. RAMSAY.
Sgt. O. L. PRATT.

Ten. Brig. do Ar Juniti Saito
Comandante da Força Aérea Brasileira
Harrowbeer, 16 de Outubro de 2009

70th Anniversary Celebrations

In 2011, the 70th Anniversary of the opening of the Airfield was celebrated with a weekend of events, including flying displays from an Air Sea Rescue Sea King Helicopter, a Fairey Swordfish (above) of the Royal Naval Historic Flight and the Battle of Britain Memorial Flight's Hurricane and Spitfire. Among the many ground displays was a replica MKIX Spitfire (below) with a working Merlin engine which was regularly run up, much to the delight of spectators.

Photos by Pavel & Marek Vincenc

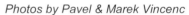